PILLOWS

PILLOWS

Created by: The Editors of Creative Publishing international, Inc.

Library of Congress Cataloging-in-Publication Data
Pillows.
    p.   cm. -- (Creative textiles)
    Includes index.
    ISBN 0-86573-410-0
    1. Pillows.   I. Creative Publishing international.   II. Series.
TT410.P55 1997
646.2'1--dc21   97-7673

THE HOME DECORATING INSTITUTE®

CONTENTS

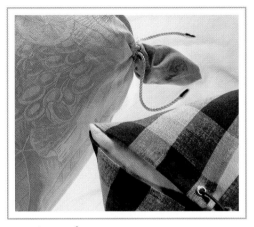

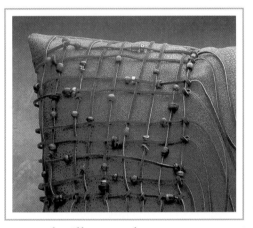

DECORATING WITH PILLOWS

*Enhance a room with pillows
that reflect your personal style.*

RTFULLY DESIGNED PILLOWS ARRANGED ON A SOFA OR BED

GIVE A ROOM COZY, INVITING AMBIENCE. THEY WAKE UP

QUIET COLORS, OFFER INTERESTING TEXTURAL VARIATIONS,

AND INTRODUCE EXTRAVAGANCE AT RELATIVELY LOW COST.

MAKING YOUR OWN PILLOWS IS NOT ONLY EASY AND AFFORDABLE,

IT ALLOWS YOU THE FREEDOM TO SELECT FABRICS AND TRIMS

IN THE COLORS, TEXTURES, AND STYLES THAT

MAKE A DECORATING SCHEME UNIQUELY YOUR OWN.

TRADITIONAL

Traditional decorating is a celebration of gracious living. The timeless beauty of classic furniture and architectural details reminiscent of a genteel past are combined in a decorating style that is also warm and comfortable. Exquisitely detailed accessories, such as antique clocks or oil paintings with intricately carved gold-leaf frames, enrich the scheme. Luxurious fabrics, such as damask, silk moiré, tapestry, needlepoint, and velvet cover the upholstered furniture and dress the windows. Decorator pillows made in these rich fabrics and accented with lavish fringes, tassels, gimps, and ornate buttons express elegance while adding a soft, inviting touch.

Traditional. A rich tapestry pillow (page 72) picks up the colors found in the printed fabric of the sofa. The striped chair fabric is repeated in the second pillow, which features a brush fringe edging (page 69). Repeating an upholstery fabric on a pillow helps to unify the room.

CONTEMPORARY

Sophistication and simplicity blend together perfectly in contemporary style. Understated background colors set the stage for clean-lined sculptural furnishings, one-of-a-kind artwork, or dramatic splashes of color. Excitement is generated by a mix of textures. Sleek hard surfaces of metal, stone, and glass contrast with nubby raw silks, supple suedes and leathers, or thick piles, each catching the eye and asking to be touched. Simple knife-edge pillows can be sewn from fabrics that bring both color and textural interest into a contemporary scheme.

Contemporary. Knife-edge pillows (page 66), in neutral prints, are accented with matching tassels and decorative welting. The neutral pillows repeat the colors found in the painting and throw, giving the room a coordinated look.

COUNTRY

Whether a romantic English garden style or a more sparsely furnished Shaker farmhouse look, country decorating always exudes friendly hospitality and reflects a casual, uncomplicated lifestyle. A valued heritage is evident in antique or handcrafted furnishings and collected memorabilia. Fabrics that bring warmth and charm to the country home may include homespun naturals in subtle hues or a mix of plaids, checks, stripes, tweeds, and floral patterns. Pillows for a country scheme can take on an antique look, using vintage fabrics like the feed-bag and quilt pillows on page 51.

Country. The welted knife-edge pillows (page 66) in this country room are made from overall prints with a country feel. Colors for the overall prints were pulled from the large floral-print fabric covering the armchair. Simple knife-edge pillows are a good style choice when combining several busy prints in a small area.

ECLECTIC

An eclectic decorating scheme is uniquely personal, combining a variety of favorite, though unrelated, furniture pieces, artwork, and accessories in one room. Mismatched elements are brought together in pleasant harmony with the creative repetition of a color, pattern, or theme common to each item. Through careful selection of fabric and style, pillows can be used in an eclectic scheme to help create that harmony. For example, an antique settee and a contemporary painting used in the same room can be linked by an arrangement of pillows echoing colors in the painting.

Eclectic. Solid-colored pillows accented with matching brush fringe (page 69) were used to create a resting point for the eye in this heavily patterned room. The solid-colored square pillows repeat the look found in the square colored tiles of the cocktail table.

COLOR MAGIC

*C*olor has more impact on the ambience of a room than any other design element. Color can visually change the size of a room, impact our perception of the room's temperature, and even arouse our emotions. Vibrant warm colors, the reds, yellows, and oranges, visually advance, making a large room appear smaller and creating a cozy atmosphere. They have the ability to energize us, agitate us, and even make us crave food. Greens, blues, and violets, the cool colors, visually recede, creating an aura of spaciousness and serenity. Small doses of color can magically unify a room, highlight favorite furnishings and artwork, or wake up a conservative color scheme.

Pillows, because of their size and versatility, offer a perfect opportunity to introduce splashes of dramatic color into a room. Add romance and sophistication to a neutral color scheme with rich jewel-toned pillows. Draw attention to a patterned rug or favorite painting by making pillows that echo its colors. To liven up a

Bright-patterned pillow *and accessories add drama and sophistication to a neutral decorating scheme.*

Plaid pillow *(left) unifies the room by combining the colors found in the wall, chair, and rug.*

monochromatic color scheme, make a pillow in a complementary color. For instance, bring a dash of sunshine into a cool blue room with cheery yellow pillows. Or tone down a vibrant red floral print by adding a few pillows that accent the cool green foliage. Make a multicolored pillow to create a relationship between several mismatched room elements. Utilize pillows to balance the color scheme in value, also. If the existing furnishings are all dark brown, for example, invigorate the room with a few pillows in tan and cream.

Look for color inspiration in lots of places, from nature to furniture stores to fashion and decorating magazines. If a particular photograph or room setting appeals to you, analyze the color strategy that first caught your eye. Then consider how that strategy could work for you. Find color samples that match the walls, floor, and furnishings in your home to help you select the pillow fabrics and coordinating trims. Determine what kind of color magic you want to create with your pillows, and finding the right fabric will be less of a challenge.

Neutral pillows in varying tones are used to create color-value interest in a neutral decorating scheme.

Geometric-patterned fabric (right) picks up colors found in other room accessories. Using color samples that match the wall color, rug, throw, and vases makes it easy to find coordinating pillow fabric.

PATTERNS & TEXTURES

Solid fabrics work well for pillows that are to be used as accents in rooms that already have a lot of pattern. Textured solids can be used to create more interest than a plain-weave solid and work especially well in contemporary interiors. Examples of textured fabrics may include chenille, crinkled fabric, quilted fabric, and matelassé. Fabrics with a tone-on-tone design, such as a damask, have subtle patterns but can often be used in place of solids.

Geometric prints and stripes work well in contemporary settings because of their simple lines and also work well

Patterned fabrics are combined successfully in the grouping of pillows above. The solid pillows repeat colors found in the tapestry pillow, and a patterned solid creates more interest than a plain-weave fabric.

in traditional and country decorating schemes when combined with floral or other prints using the same colors.

Overall prints and florals are often used in traditional and country decorating schemes and, depending on the feel of the design, may be used in contemporary settings. Many ethnic-inspired prints, mosaics, and exotic prints also have overall designs.

Metallics provide sheen and are easily used in traditional, contemporary, and eclectic interiors. Metallic fabrics or fabrics with some metallic threads give a formal look to a room. Consider underlining a sheer metallic to create

Texture adds dimension to both solid and multicolored fabrics, as shown in the simple pillows at left.

a solid with more interest. Metallic fabrics can be used to help unify a room that has other metallic accessories, such as candlesticks or picture frames.

FABRIC SELECTION

When selecting fabrics for pillows, consider how the pillow will be used. If the pillow is to be used in a low-traffic room and will mainly serve as a decorator accent, then elegant fabrics and trims may work well. For pillows that will be frequently used and may

Geometric patterned fabrics are used for pillows (right) with coordinating twisted welting trim.

require repeated laundering, select fabrics that will hold up to the wear and tear.

As a general rule, the tighter the weave or higher the thread count (number of threads per inch), the stronger the fabric. For durability, also look for fabrics treated with stain-resistant or water-resistant finishes.

Protective finishes should be reapplied after laundering or dry cleaning. You can apply protective finishes yourself with a spray available at fabric stores. Or a dry cleaner can usually apply the finish for you.

Metallic threads add sheen to knife-edge pillows (left). Decorative cording finished with metal end caps adds detailing to the pillows.

BE YOUR OWN DESIGNER

Pillows are an excellent way to add accent colors or unusual textures to your decorating scheme. Nestled on sofas and armchairs, pillows help create a warm, inviting atmosphere. The small amounts of materials needed for pillows make it affordable to use lavish fabrics and trims for a touch of elegance and sophistication, even in casual rooms.

Pillows can be embellished with a variety of trims to enhance both casual and elegant styles. Choose from simple, self-fabric welting or elegant braid trims, fringe, or tassels. Even decorative buttons, beads, or charms can be used for embellishment. Select the trims that reflect your own personal style.

Many of the pillows in this book will work in any decorating scheme. The easy bolster pillows on page 57 have a romantic country look, but by substituting silk fabric and luxurious trims they could easily work in a formal traditional living room. Even though the tapestry pillows on page 77 have an opulent look, they are basically sewn like the feed-bag pillows on page 51. To use any of the pillows in this book in any decorating scheme, simply choose fabrics and trims that coordinate in style with the other furnishings in the room.

Decorative pillow trims shown at left include tassels, decorative buttons, gimp trim, beads, looped fringe, and twisted welting.

FORMS & FILLINGS

Pillows get their shape from forms or loose fillings. Depending on their washability, loose fillings may be stuffed directly into the pillow covering or encased in a separate liner for easy removal. For ease in laundering or dry cleaning, make a separate inner covering or liner for the stuffing, using lightweight muslin or lining fabric, or use purchased pillow forms. Make the liner as you would a knife-edge pillow (pages 66 to 68), fill it with stuffing, and machine-stitch it closed. Choose from several kinds of forms and fillings.

Standard polyester forms are square, round, and rectangular, for knife-edge pillows in sizes from 10" to 30" (25.5 to 76 cm). These forms are nonallergenic, washable, do not bunch, and may have muslin or polyester outer coverings.

Polyester fiberfill is a washable, nonallergenic filling for pillows or pillow liners. Fiberfill comes in loose-pack bags or pressed into batting sheets of varying densities. For a smooth pillow, sew an inner liner of batting, then stuff with loose fill. Soften the hard edges of polyurethane foam by wrapping the foam with batting.

Kapok is a vegetable-fiber filling, favored by some decorators because of its softness. However, kapok is messy to work with and becomes matted with use.

Down is washed, quill-less feathers from the breasts of geese and ducks. Down makes the most luxurious pillows, and it is expensive.

CASUAL PILLOW *S*TYLES

INFORMAL & EXPRESSIVE.

SIMPLE & RELAXED.

Flanged & Fringed
PILLOWS

Flanged or fringed decorator pillows
can be put together in a snap. Soft,
supple leathers and suedes can be
made into rich flanged or fringed pillows
for a living room or den. Synthetic
leathers and suedes may be used as
well. Or, for less expense, a more casual
look can be achieved by making cozy
fringed pillows from reversible polyester
fleece fabric.

To make the flanged pillows, leather lacing
is threaded through holes that have been
punched in the leather, securing the pillow
front to the back. For a finishing touch, decorative buttons or conchos are tied to the corners. The tools and materials needed can be
purchased at leather craft and supply stores.

Because leather, suede, and fleece do not ravel,
fringed pillows are made simply by sewing and
cutting. The look can be varied by lengthening
or shortening the fringe, or by tying a row of
knots in the fringe at the stitching line.

*Suede pillow with knotted fringe (opposite), is paired
with a leather flanged pillow for a luxurious look.*

LIST *of* MATERIALS

- ► Pillow form in desired size.
- ► Soft leather or suede, or synthetic leather or suede.
- ► Leather lacing.
- ► Leather lacing needle; needlenose pliers.
- ► Hole punch tool, in size appropriate for lacing; wooden or rubber mallet; cutting mat.
- ► Four conchos or decorative buttons.

CUTTING DIRECTIONS

Determine the desired depth of the flange, from 2" to 3½" (5 to 9 cm), depending on the size of the pillow. Cut pillow front and pillow back, with sides equal to the measurements of the pillow form plus twice the desired depth of the flange.

Cut four leather lacing strips, with lengths equal to the length of one side of the pillow form plus 10" (25.5 cm).

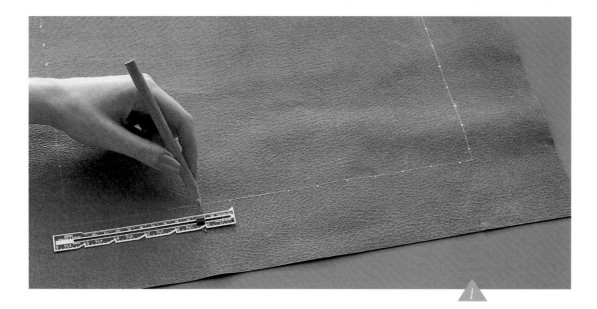

1...... Mark depth of the flange with faint pencil line on wrong side of the pillow front. Mark dots for the holes along pencil line, spacing the marks 1" (2.5 cm) apart and beginning and ending 1/2" (1.3 cm) from each corner. There should be an even number of marks on each side.

2...... Place pillow front over the pillow back, aligning edges, right sides together on cutting mat. Punch holes at the marks, using punching tool and mallet.

continued

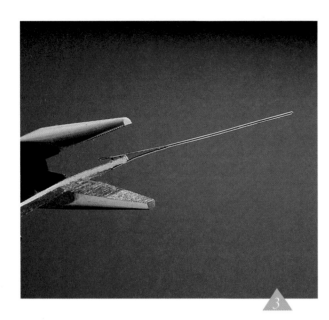

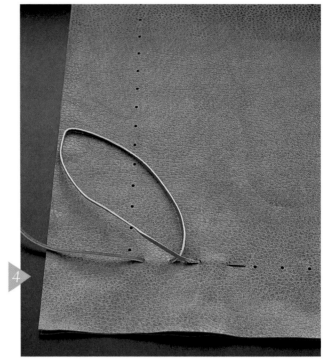

3...... Open leather needle at spring end; insert lacing, with top side of lacing against prongs. Using the needlenose pliers, squeeze needle so prongs pierce lacing.

4...... Place pillow front over pillow back, wrong sides together, aligning edges and holes. Beginning at one corner, insert lacing through aligned holes from front to back; bring lacing up through next set of holes.

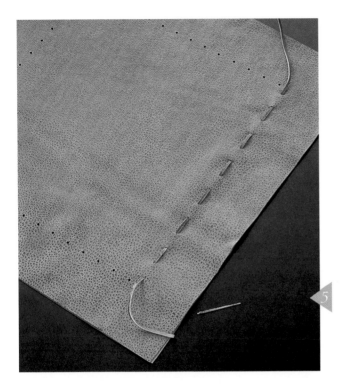

5...... Continue lacing to last set of holes on one side; leave tails of equal length at beginning and end of side. Remove lacing from needle.

6...... Repeat steps 3 to 5 for two more sides. Insert the pillow form into open side; lace the open side shut.

7...... Lace tails through concho or button at corner, if desired; tie square knot. Repeat for all corners.

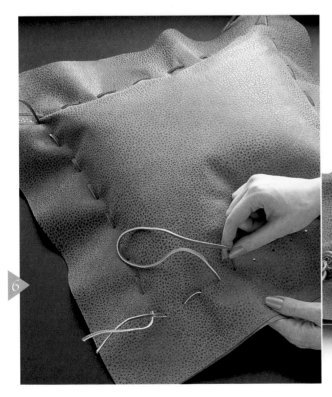

LIST *of* MATERIALS

▶ Soft leather or suede, synthetic leather or suede, or reversible polyester fleece.

▶ Pillow form in desired size.

▶ Narrow masking tape.

CUTTING DIRECTIONS

Determine the desired depth of the fringe, from 2" to 3½" (5 to 9 cm), depending on the size of the pillow. Cut pillow front and pillow back, with sides equal to the measurements of the pillow form plus twice the desired depth of the fringe.

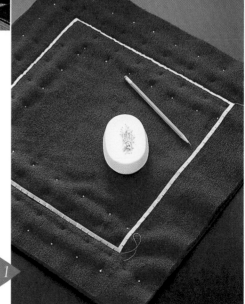

1 . . . . . . Place the pillow front over the pillow back, wrong sides together, matching edges. Mark length of the fringe on all sides, using narrow masking tape. Mark desired width of fringe strips on tape, ½" (1.3 cm) for fleece, ⅜" to ½" (1 to 1.3 cm) for suede or leather. secure layers together, using pins for fleece or paper clips for suede or leather. Sew three sides, using walking foot, if available.

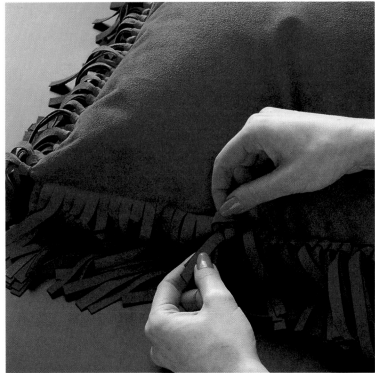

2...... Cut fringe on sewn sides, using rotary cutter and cutting board. Use straightedge as guide, cutting to within ½" (1.3 cm) of the tape. Finish cutting, with scissors, up to, but not through, the stitching.

3...... Insert pillow form; sew remaining side. Cut fringe on remaining side. Remove tape.

Optional knots. Grasp first set of fringe strips; tie together in overhand knot, securing knot tightly at stitching. Continue tying knots on all sides; for uniform appearance, tie all knots in the same direction.

Laced Leather
PILLOWS

For laced pillows, select soft, supple leather or suede; a synthetic leather or suede may also be used. The leather skins and any necessary supplies are available at leather craft and supply stores. For the laced edges of pillows, leather and suede lacing is available in various widths. To determine the amount of lacing needed for a laced pillow, allow about three times the distance to be laced, plus 1 1/4 yd. (1.15 m) for knotted ends.

A punch tool and mallet are used to make lacing holes in leather quickly and easily. Punch tools are available in many sizes; a size 4, or 5/32" (3.8 mm), punch tool will work for most lacing. When punching leather, work on a hard, smooth surface, such as a sturdy workbench or a piece of firm Masonite® or marble. A pencil may be used for marking lacing holes that will be punched out of the leather.

Special leather stains are available in several shades. They not only change the color of a vegetable-tanned leather, they also bring out the grain. Before applying stain to a project, test it on a scrap of the leather you will be using. If stain is being applied to a lightweight leather, some shrinkage may occur. Leather finishes are also available; they provide a durable, water-repellent finish and a soft luster.

LACED LEATHER PILLOW

LIST *of* MATERIALS

- Leather.
- Leather lacing.
- Leather round-drive punch tool, in size appropriate for lacing; a size 4, or 5/32" (3.8 mm), will work for most leather lacing.
- Leather-lacing needle; needlenose pliers.

- Mallet, of wood, rubber, or rawhide.
- Mat knife or rotary cutter; metal straightedge.
- Pillow form, in desired size.
- Decorative beads, optional.
- Leather stain, optional.
- Leather finish.

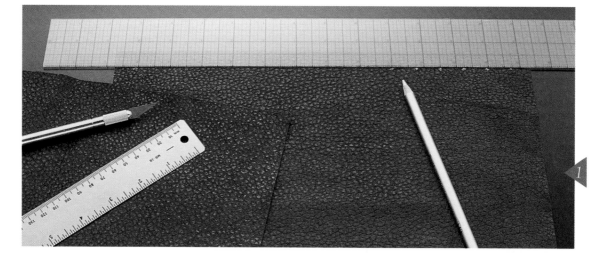

1...... Cut pillow front and pillow back from leather, using metal straight-edge and mat knife or rotary cutter, cutting them 1" (2.5 cm) wider and longer than pillow form. Using chalk or pencil, mark placement for lacing holes on top side of pillow front, 5/8" (1.5 cm) from edges; position a hole at each corner and at intervals of 3/4" to 1" (2 to 2.5 cm).

2...... Punch holes for lacing in pillow front, using punch tool and mallet. Place pillow front and pillow back with top sides together. Using the pillow front as a guide, mark holes on the top side of the pillow back. Punch holes.

3...... Cut a length of leather lacing equal to three times the length of first side to be laced plus 12" (30.5 cm). Using mat knife, trim end of lacing to a point. Thread leather needle with lacing as on page 20, step 3.

4...... Place pillow front and pillow back with top sides facing out. Using whipstitch, lace first side; leave about 6" (15 cm) tails at ends. Repeat to lace three sides of pillow.

5...... Insert pillow form. Lace remaining side. Tie ends of lacing at corners. Attach beads, if desired, securing them with overhand knot.

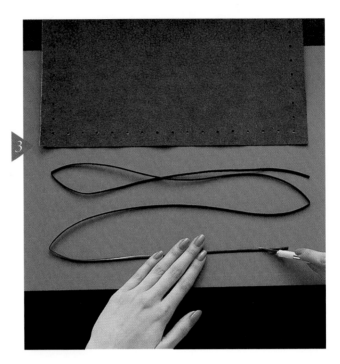

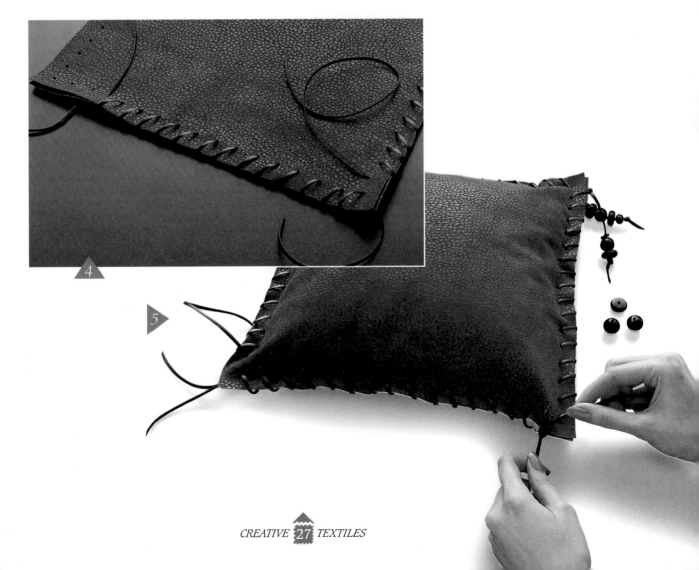

Strips of leather are pieced together on the diagonal for this pillow front. Overlap the strips, and stitch, using a leather needle. Or glue the strips, using a leather cement.

Animal skin is used for the front of a laced pillow. Mark and punch the holes from the back side of the skin.

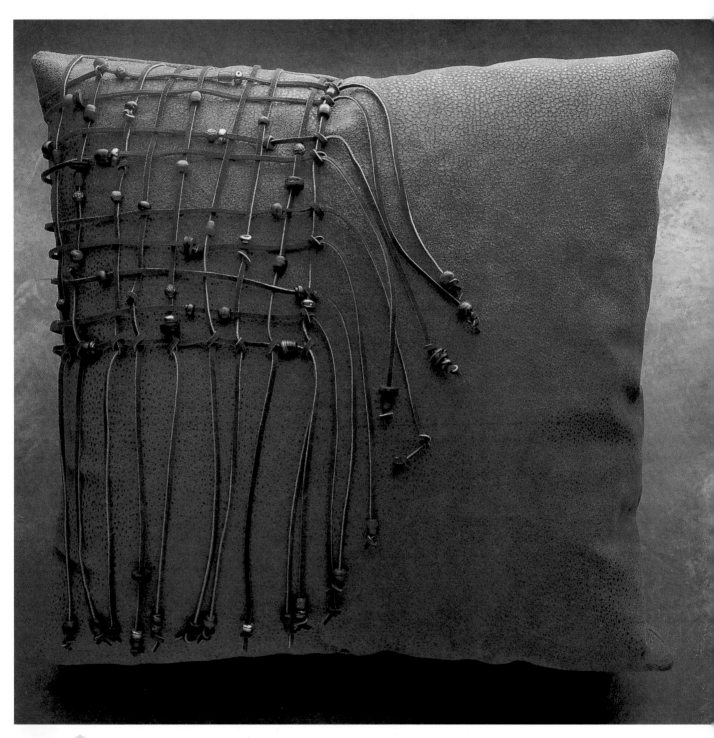

Leather lacing strips, woven together, are inserted into the seams at one corner of the pillow above. Beads, woven in randomly, add color.

Haberdashery
PILLOWS

For a unique accent, create a pillow from men's discarded suits. Nestled among traditional pillows, a haberdashery pillow adds an unexpected touch of whimsy. The instructions starting on page 32 are for a trapezoid-shaped pillow about 16" (40.5 cm) high.

Old suits are readily available at secondhand stores or garage sales. Look for jackets with interesting details. Pockets, buttonholes, and manufacturer's labels add interest to the pillow. Do not overlook lining fabrics and lining details. From the suit pants, welted back pockets, portions of the waistband, and the fly front can be used. A necktie may also be used as an accent.

HABERDASHERY PILLOW

LIST of MATERIALS

▶ Men's suit coat; suit pants or necktie, optional.

▶ Muslin, for underlining.

▶ Purchased welting, if desired.

▶ Lightweight paper, for pattern.

▶ Polyester fiberfill.

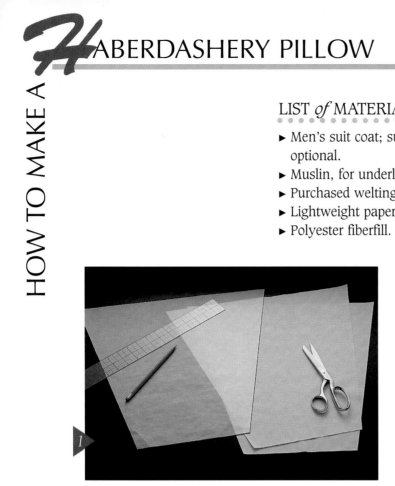

1 ...... Draw 18½" (47.3 cm) line on paper; draw a parallel 9" (23 cm) line centered 17" (43 cm) below first line. Draw connecting lines to make pattern, which includes ½" (1.3 cm) seam allowances. Cut two underlining pieces from muslin, using pattern.

2 ...... Plan placement of major design details for pillow front, such as lapels and pockets, by placing muslin over the garment; mark garment with chalk, and trace design details onto muslin.

3 ...... Cut design pieces from garment, adding ½" (1.3 cm) seam allowances. Cut pieces from the outer layer of the garment only; this allows you to use the lining details for other areas of pillow.

4..... Plan placement of smaller pieces, incorporating details such as lining pockets and garment labels. Cut pieces, adding ½" (1.3 cm) seam allowances.

5..... Arrange fabric pieces in desired placement; set aside the lapel piece. Stitch remaining pieces to the underlining, using stitch-and-flip and edgestitch methods on page 35. If desired, smaller pieces may be seamed together into larger units before securing them to the underlining.

6..... Attach lapel piece by stitching under the lapel, about ¼" (6 mm) from the roll line.

continued

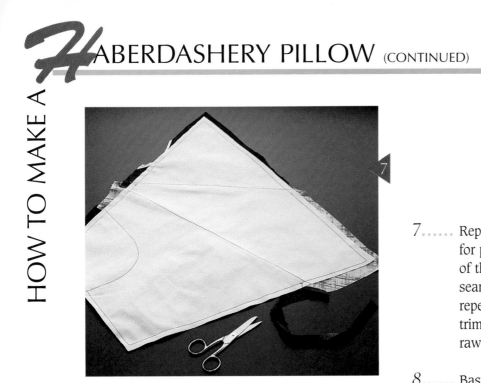

7...... Repeat steps 2 to 5 on pages 32 and 33 for pillow back. Baste around outer edges of the pillow front, within ½" (1.3 cm) seam allowances of muslin underlining; repeat for pillow back. From both pieces, trim excess fabric that extends beyond raw edges of the underlining.

8...... Baste welting, if desired, to the pillow front, along one or more seams; tape ends of welting into seam allowance. Pin pillow front to pillow back, right sides together. Stitch ½" (1.3 cm) seam around pillow, leaving opening on one side for turning.

9...... Turn pillow right side out, pulling out corners. Press under seam allowances of opening. Stuff the pillow with fiberfill. Slipstitch or edgestitch opening closed.

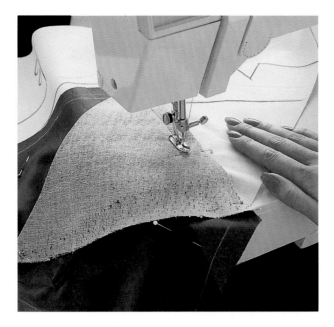

Stitch-and-flip method. 1. Apply any garment pieces that have raw edges by placing one piece on muslin underlining; pin in place. Place a second piece on the first piece, right sides together, aligning raw edges. Stitch ½" (1.3 cm) from aligned edges.

2....... Flip top garment piece right side up; press. Pin in place. Continue attaching pieces, pressing under ½" (1.3 cm) seam allowance on any raw edges that will not be covered by another piece.

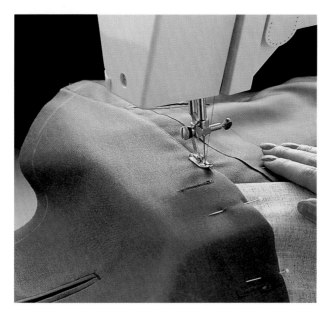

Edgestitch method. Apply any pieces that have finished edges, such as the garment front edge, by stitching them to the muslin underlining close to the finished edge of each piece.

Men's shirt is used for the haberdashery pillow with a necktie added for an accent of color. Men's suit trousers are used for the rectangular pillow, above right. Details include the welted back pocket, the fly front, and the pants cuffs; suspenders were also added.

MORE IDEAS FOR
Haberdashery
PILLOWS

School band uniform, a memento of school activities, makes a unique haberdashery pillow.

Rag Rug
PILLOWS

Inexpensive rag rugs can be easily transformed into decorator pillows with appealing texture. Made from large rugs, these pillows can be used as comfortable floor pillows, providing additional seating in a family room; from small rugs, they make accent pillows for the sofa. Because the finished size of a rag rug pillow depends on the size of the rug, you may not be able to use a purchased pillow form. If a purchased pillow form is not available in the size you need, make your own form by stitching together two layers of polyester upholstery batting and then stuffing polyester fiberfill between the layers. Or, in some cases, you may find a bed pillow that fits.

LIST *of* MATERIALS

▶ Woven rag rug.

▶ Heavy-duty thread, such as pearl cotton or button and carpet thread; large-eyed needle.

▶ Purchased pillow form in desired size; or polyester upholstery batting and polyester fiberfill, to make a pillow form.

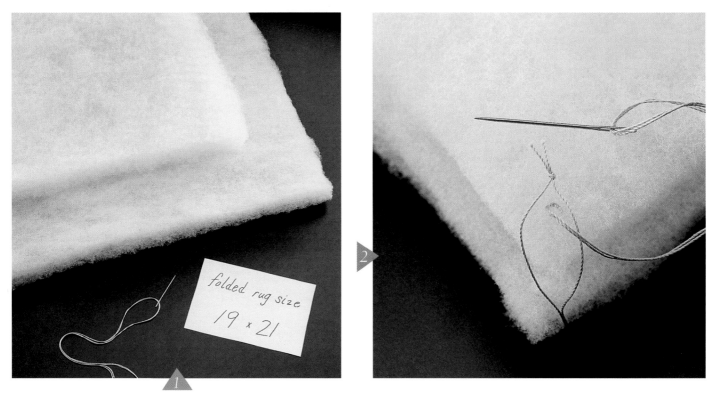

folded rug size
19 x 21

1 ...... Cut two pieces of polyester upholstery batting to the desired finished size of the pillow. Thread a large-eyed needle with a double strand of heavy thread; knot end.

2 ...... Layer the two pieces of batting. At one corner, run the needle through both layers and then between the threads, above the knot. Pull tight.

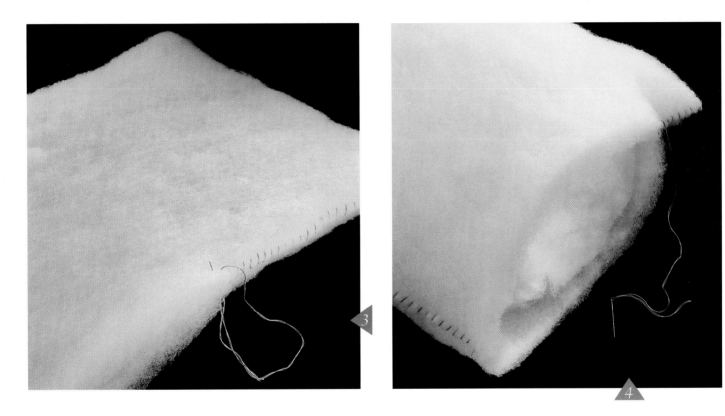

3...... Whipstitch the layers together along three sides. Knot thread securely each time you run out of thread, and begin again by securing the thread as in step 2.

4...... Stuff form with polyester fiberfill to desired fullness. Whipstitch the last side closed. Knot thread securely.

RAG RUG PILLOW

1...... Fold the rag rug in half, aligning
the fringed ends; pin. Thread a
large-eyed needle with a double
strand of heavy thread. Stitch
fringed ends of rug together,
taking 1/4"(6 mm) stitches.

2...... Refold the stitched rug so the
fringe is about one-third the
distance from the top fold. Turn
fringe toward the bottom fold.

3...... Stitch folded rug together along one side, using a double strand of heavy thread. Mark opposite side of rug at top and bottom folds.

4...... Insert pillow form (page 40). Stitch the open side closed, folding top and bottom of rug at marked points. Knot securely.

Mock Box
PILLOWS

Mock box pillows are easy to make, with pleated corners that are simply folded in place. Suitable for any decorating style, the pillows may be plain or trimmed with welting. Large pillows can be stacked for use as floor pillows, or smaller ones used as accent pillows.

Pillow forms are available in many sizes, up to 30" (76 cm) square. They vary in price, depending on the amount and type of filling used and on the quality of the cover fabric. For economy, you can use pillow forms filled with polyester fiberfill; the down pillow forms are more expensive.

If desired, you can make your own pillow forms inexpensively by stitching together two layers of polyester upholstery batting and then stuffing polyester fiberfill between the layers of batting as on pages 40 and 41. By making your own pillow forms you are able to create them in dimensions that may not be available ready-made.

LIST *of* MATERIALS

► Fabric, for pillow front and back.

► Contrasting fabric and cording, for optional welting.

► Purchased pillow form, or polyester upholstery batting and polyester fiberfill if you are making the pillow form. The length of the form is equal to the combined measurements of the desired length and thickness of the finished pillow; the width of the form is equal to the combined measurements of the desired width and thickness of the finished pillow.

CUTTING DIRECTIONS

For the pillow front and pillow back, cut two pieces of fabric, 1" (2.5 cm) longer than the desired finished length of the pillow plus the desired finished thickness, or loft, of the pillow. The cut width of the pillow front and pillow back is 1" (2.5 cm) wider than the desired finished width of the pillow plus the desired finished thickness.

If you are making the pillow form, cut two batting pieces, with the length of the pieces equal to the desired finished length of the pillow plus the desired finished thickness, or loft, of the pillow. The cut width of the batting pieces is equal to the desired finished width of the pillow plus the desired finished thickness.

If welting is desired, cut fabric strips on the bias; for economical use of fabric, the strips may be cut at an angle less than 45°. To determine how wide to cut the strips, wrap a piece of fabric around the cording, pinning it together. Measure this distance, and add 1" (2.5 cm) for seam allowances. Cut the bias fabric strips for the welting to this width; the combined length of the fabric strips is equal to the distance around the pillow plus extra for seam allowances.

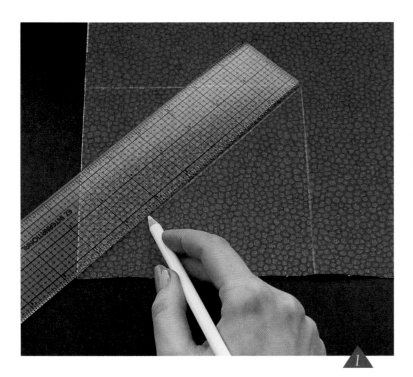

1 ...... Mark a square on the right side of the fabric at one corner, using chalk, with each side of the square measuring one-half of the desired thickness of the finished pillow plus ½" (1.3 cm). Draw a diagonal line through the square, ending at corner of fabric.

2 ...... Fold fabric on the marked lines of the square, bringing the folds to the diagonal line. Pin in place.

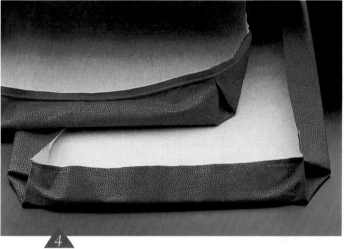

3...... Baste across the pleats within the ½" (1.3 cm) seam allowance. Trim off triangular section of excess fabric at the corner.

4...... Repeat steps 1 to 3 for all corners of pillow front and pillow back. If welting is desired, make and apply the welting as on page 49, steps 1 to 5.

5...... Pin the pillow front to the pillow back, right sides together, matching corner tucks. Stitch around pillow in ½" (1.3 cm) seam, leaving an opening on one side for turning. If pillow has welting, use a zipper foot and stitch inside previous stitching line, crowding stitches against the welting.

continued

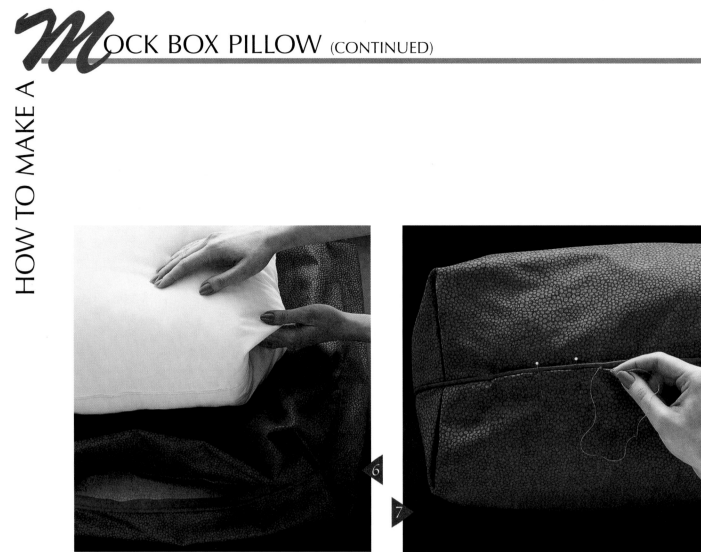

6...... Turn the pillow right side out through opening. Use purchased pillow form, or make pillow form as on pages 40 and 41, steps 1 to 4. Punch in corners of the pillow form, and insert it into mock box pillow cover.

7...... Slipstitch the opening closed.

HOW TO MAKE & APPLY THE *Welting*

1...... Cut the fabric strips (page 46); seam the strips together as necessary for the desired length. Fold the fabric strip around the cording, wrong sides together, matching raw edges. Using a zipper foot, machine-baste close to cording; smooth cording twists.

2...... Stitch welting to the right side of fabric, over previous stitches, matching raw edges and starting 2" (5 cm) from the end of the welting; clip and ease welting at corners.

3...... Stop stitching 2" (5 cm) from the point where ends of welting will meet. Cut off one end of welting so it overlaps the other end by 1" (2.5 cm).

4...... Remove the stitching from one end of the welting, and trim ends of the cording so they just meet.

5...... Fold under ½" (1.3 cm) of fabric on overlapping end of welting. Lap it around the other end; finish stitching welting to pillow front.

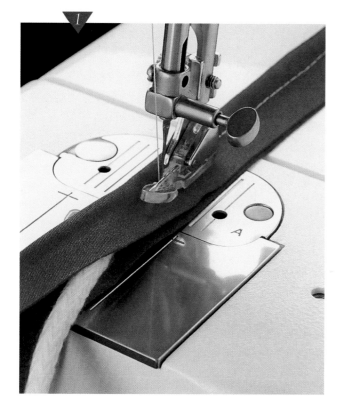

Feed-bag Pillows
WITH QUILT BORDERS

Feed bags and quilts are popular collectibles. Together, they make charming pillows. The feed bag works well as a creative inset, and the quilt can be cut into strips for the border. Use the remaining scraps from either the feed bag or the quilt for the back of the pillow.

Authentic old feed bags can be readily found at antique stores, and reproductions of the originals may be found at flea markets. Also available are seed bags and flour sacks, which work equally well for pillow insets. For the quilt border, it is not necessary to find a perfect quilt. A more affordable unfinished, damaged, or even stained quilt may be used, because only a small amount of quilted fabric is needed.

A down pillow form is used to make this practical pillow especially soft and comfortable. A large pillow form, 22" to 28" (56 to 71 cm) square, is recommended, in order to feature both the printing on the feed bag and the piecework of the quilt. For best results, the feed-bag inset should measure about two-thirds of the pillow form. On 22" to 28" (56 to 71 cm) pillows, insets generally range from 14" to 18" (35.5 to 46 cm), with borders from 4" to 5" (10 to 12.5 cm).

LIST *of* MATERIALS

▶ Feed bag; seed bag or flour sack may be substituted.
▶ Quilt.
▶ Down pillow form.

CUTTING DIRECTIONS

For the feed-bag inset, cut a square of fabric from the front of the feed bag, 1" (2.5 cm) larger than the desired finished size of the inset; center the logo or printing from side to side and from top to bottom. The border strips and pillow back are cut during the construction process, in the following steps.

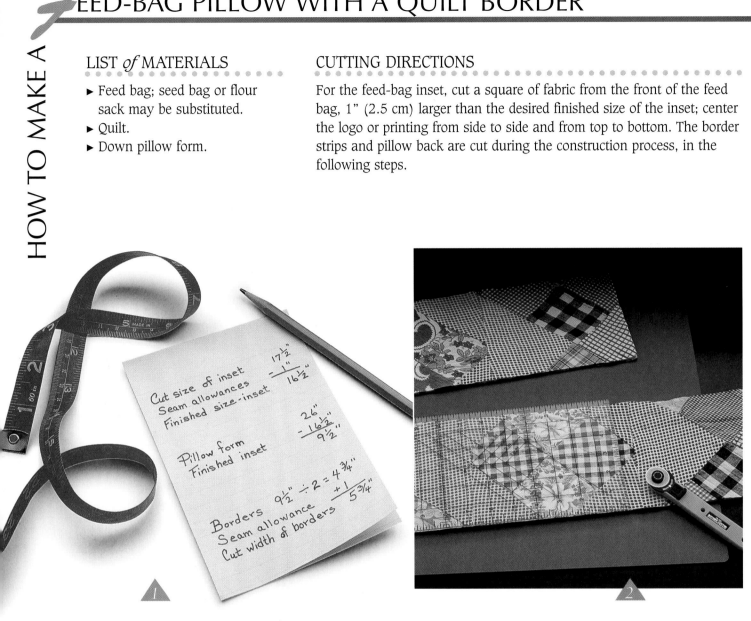

1 ...... Subtract the finished size of the inset from the size of the pillow form; divide this measurement by two. Then add 1" (2.5 cm) to determine the cut width of the border strips.

2 ...... Cut two border strips from the quilt to the cut width determined in step 1; the cut length of the strips is equal to the cut width of the inset.

3...... Stitch one border strip to the upper edge of inset, right sides together, stitching ½" (1.3 cm) seam. Stitch the second strip to lower edge of inset. Press seam allowances toward the inset.

4...... Cut two remaining border strips from the quilt to the same cut width as previous border strips; the cut length of each of these strips is equal to the side measurement, including the borders.

continued

HOW TO MAKE A

5...... Stitch one border strip to each side, right sides together, stitching ½" (1.3 cm) seams. Press the seam allowances toward the inset.

6...... Use scraps from feed bag or quilt for the pillow back, piecing as necessary. Pin pillow front to pieced fabric for pillow back, right sides together. Using pillow front as a pattern, cut the pillow back.

7...... Stitch ½" (1.3 cm) seam around the pillow, leaving an opening on one side for turning; press seam open. At opening, press back the seam allowances. Trim the corners diagonally.

8...... Turn the pillow cover right side out, pulling out the corners.

9...... Insert the pillow form, pushing the corners of the pillow form into corners of pillow cover. Slipstitch the opening closed.

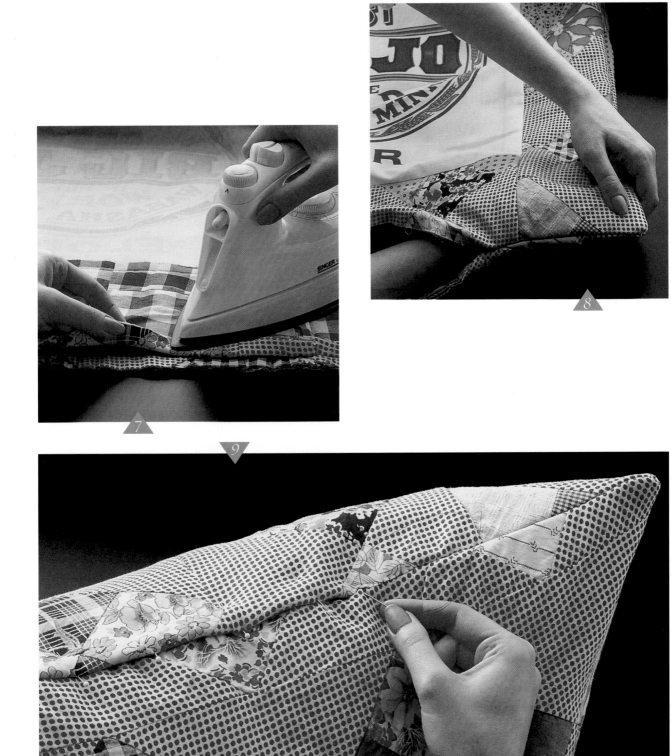

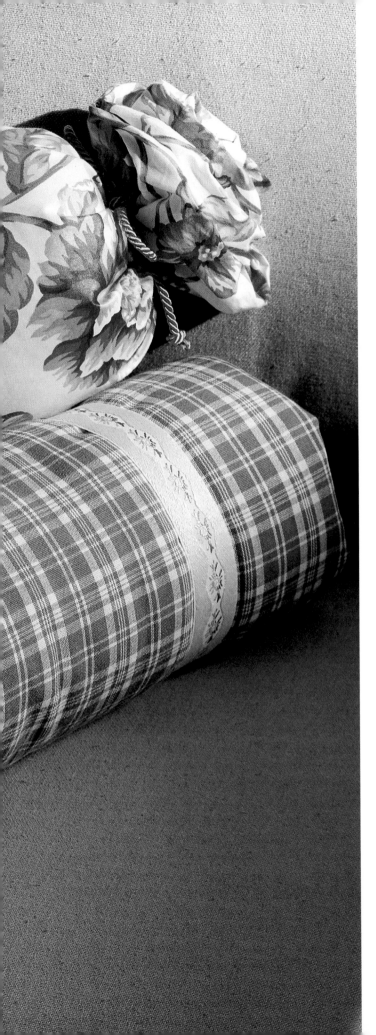

Easy Bolster
PILLOWS

Create plump bolster pillows in a matter of minutes, without sewing a single stitch. Simply wrap, roll, and tie to make these unique accent pillows for the bed or sofa. For a tailored, clean look, make jelly-roll bolsters. Just as the name implies, the ends of this pillow style look like a jelly roll. Or roll up romantic bolsters with rich rosettes tied at each end.

Bolster styles include the rosette bolster (left, top) and the jelly-roll bolster (left, bottom and below).

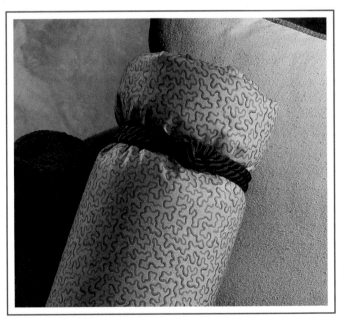

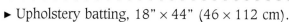

- Decorator fabric, 54" (137 cm) wide; for jelly-roll bolster, 1 yd. (0.95 m) if fabric is solid color or nondirectional print, or 1½ yd. (1.4 m) if fabric has directional print; for rosette bolster, 1½ yd. (1.4 m).

- Upholstery batting, 18" × 44" (46 × 112 cm).
- Strong string.
- 2 yd. (1.85 m) decorative cord or ribbon, cut in half.

HOW TO MAKE A *JELLY-ROLL BOLSTER*

CUTTING DIRECTIONS

Cut the fabric to a width of 36" (91.5 cm), if it has a directional print.

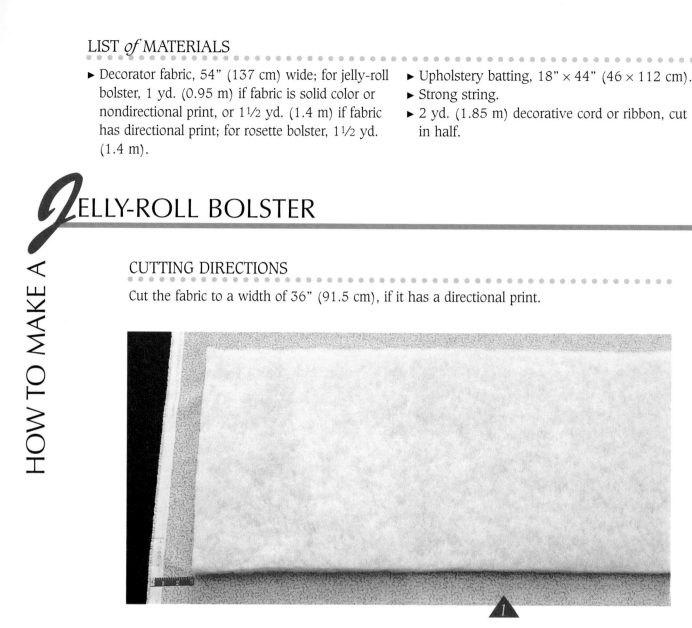

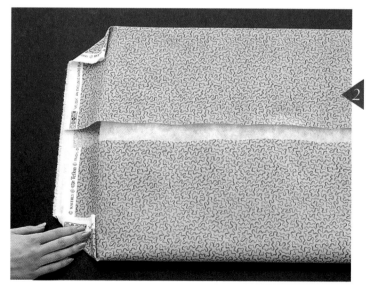

1 ...... Place fabric facedown on work surface. Place upholstery batting over fabric, centering the width of the batting over the width of the fabric, with one short end of batting 3" (7.5 cm) from end of fabric.

2 ...... Wrap the long edges of fabric in over the batting. Miter the fabric ends; wrap ends in over batting.

3...... Roll wrapped batting, beginning at end with shorter mitered wrap. Keep fabric snug to batting, and roll with a firmness that does not crush the loft of the batting.

4...... Tie string snugly around bolster about 3" (7.5 cm) from each end. Wrap cord or ribbon around bolster over the string; tie knot or bow as desired, positioning bow or knot on side opposite the end of the roll.

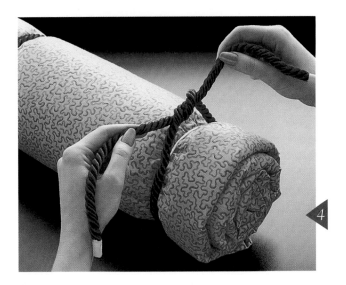

HOW TO MAKE A ROSETTE BOLSTER

1...... Follow steps 1 and 2 opposite, wrapping fabric over the batting so edges meet at the center of the batting, with equal extensions of folded fabric at each side. Follow step 3, above.

2...... Tie the string tightly at ends of the bolster, just beyond the batting. Tie cord or ribbon over the string as desired. Arrange rosettes at ends of bolster.

*Large dinner napkins become an instant slipcover for a 16"
(40.5 cm) pillow form.
Simply place the pillow form between two nap-kins and tie the corners with decorative cord or ribbons.*

Plain knife-edge pillow (right) is given a face-lift with a diagonal wrap. Grommets are inserted at each corner of a napkin, and corners are tied together over the front of the pillow, using leather lacing.

Collar effect is created by turning back the edges of a reversible napkin at each corner, revealing more of the pillow.

Tip. Tie corners of the napkins tightly with heavy thread before attaching cord or ribbon.

ELEGANT PILLOW STYLES

ORNATE & REFINED.

ARTISTIC & STYLIZED.

Decorator
PILLOWS

Decorator pillows are an inexpensive way to use lavish fabrics and trims for a touch of elegance and sophistication in your decorating scheme.

Knife-edge pillows are quick to make; a simple stitched closure allows the pillow to be decorative on both sides. If desired, emphasize the edges of the pillow by attaching a fringe; most fringes have a decorative heading and may be hand-stitched in place. Another way to trim a pillow is by inserting a twisted welting into the seam at the edges of the pillow. If you select a twisted welting that twists in the opposite direction from the welting shown on pages 70 and 71, interchange the words "left" and "right" in steps 2 to 4.

A variety of other trims, such as braid and gimp, may be applied to the front of a decorator pillow. These trims may be topstitched onto the pillow front before the pillow is assembled.

LIST *of* MATERIALS

- ▶ Decorator fabric.
- ▶ Pillow form.
- ▶ Polyester fiberfill, for filling out corners.
- ▶ Decorative trim, such as twisted welting or fringe, optional.

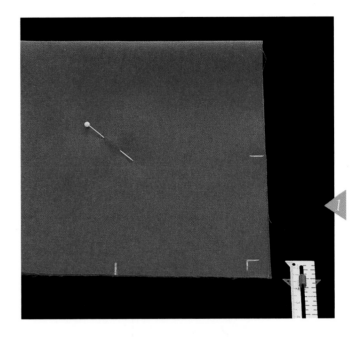

1 ...... Cut pillow front and pillow back 1" (2.5 cm) wider and longer than the pillow form. Fold the pillow front into fourths. Mark a point halfway between corner and fold on each open side. At the corner, mark a point ½" (1.3 cm) from each raw edge.

2 ...... Mark lines, tapering from the raw edges at center marks to marks at corner. Cut on marked lines.

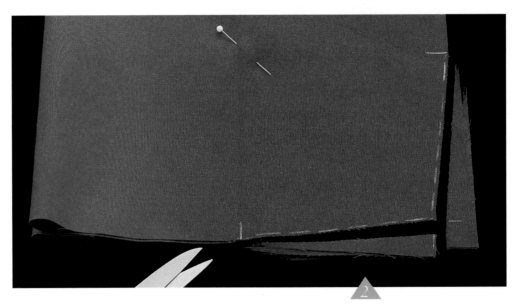

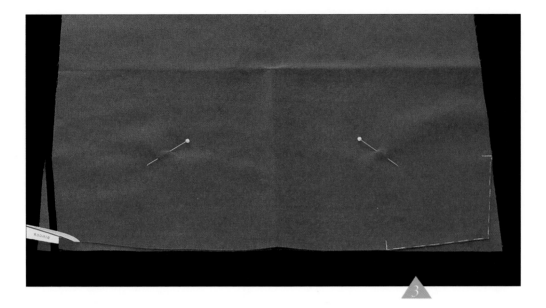

3...... Use the pillow front as pattern for cutting the pillow back so all corners are tapered. This will eliminate dog-eared corners on the finished pillow.

4...... Pin the pillow front to the pillow back, right sides together. Stitch ½" (1.3 cm) seam, leaving opening on one side for turning and for inserting the pillow form.

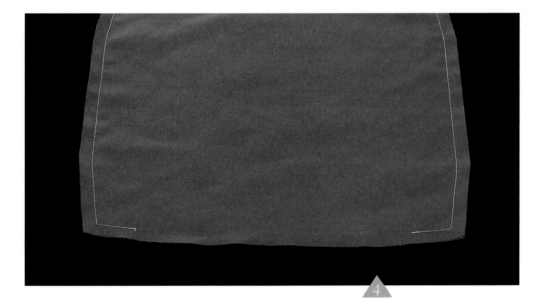

continued

HOW TO MAKE A

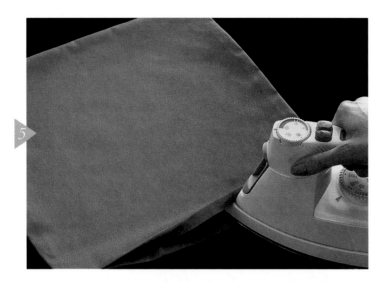

5...... Turn pillow cover right side out, pulling out the corners. Press under the seam allowances at the opening.

6...... Insert pillow form; push fiberfill into the corners of the pillow as necessary to fill out pillow.

7...... Pin opening closed; slipstitch or edgestitch close to folded edge.

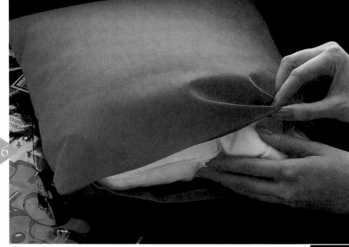

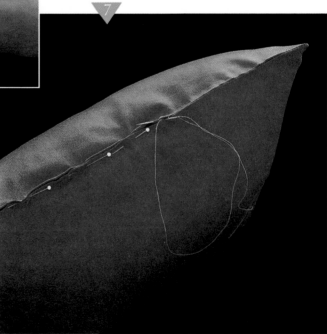

Trim without decorative heading. Machine-baste trim to right side of pillow front, with heading of fringe within seam allowance. At ends, cut fringe between loops and hand-stitch loop to secure it; butt ends together. Place pillow front and pillow back right sides together; machine-stitch. Insert pillow form.

Trim with decorative heading. Pin trim around outer edge of pillow cover; miter heading at corners by folding trim at an angle. Hand-stitch along both edges of the trim and along the diagonal fold of mitered corners. Insert pillow form.

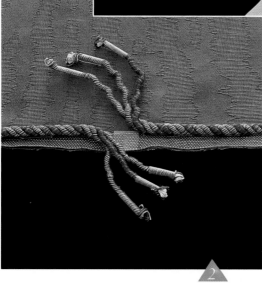

1 . . . . . . Identify right side of twisted welting; from right side, inner edge of tape is not visible. Stitch twisted welting to pillow back, using zipper foot, with right sides up and outer edge of welting tape aligned to raw edge of fabric. Leave 1½" (3.8 cm) unstitched between the ends; leave 3" (7.5 cm) tails.

2 . . . . . . Remove stitching from welting tape on tails. Separate the cords; wrap transparent tape around the ends to prevent raveling. Trim ends of the welting tape to 1" (2.5 cm) from stitching; overlap the ends, and secure with transparent tape. Arrange the cords so those at right turn up and those at left turn down.

3 . . . . . . Insert cords at right end under the welting tape, twisting them and pulling them down until the welting is returned to its original shape. Secure in place, using tape or pins.

4...... Twist and pull cords at left end over cords at right end until the twisted ends look like continuous twisted welting; check both sides of the welting.

5...... Position zipper foot on left side of needle; this will allow you to stitch in the direction of the twists. Machine-baste through all layers to secure the welting at the seamline. Cords may be hand-basted in place, if desired.

6...... Place pillow back on pillow front, right sides together. Stitch as close to the welting as possible, using zipper foot; leave opening for turning. With pillow front facing up, stitch again, crowding stitches closer to welting.

MORE IDEAS FOR
Decorator PILLOWS

Long, twisted fringe drapes gracefully along the sides of the rectangular pillow above.

Decorative panels enhance the pillows opposite. One pillow features a center fabric panel accented with antique lace and buttons; another has a purchased tapestry panel. Gimp, topstitched over the edges, frames the panels.

continued

Banded inset is the focal point of the velveteen pillow shown above. For added detail, twisted welting edges the pillow, and tassels adorn the corners.

Luxurious tassels add an elegant touch to the corners of simple pillows.

Decorative cording, cinched and tied around the simple knife-edge pillows above, adds detailing. The ends of the cording are finished with end caps.

Tapestry
PILLOWS WITH DECORATIVE TRIMS

Antique shops often have tapestries with exquisite designs. Even if a portion of the tapestry has been damaged or stained, the remainder can be salvaged. Transformed into luxurious pillows with decorative trims, these lovely tapestries make one-of-a-kind room accessories. The tapestry pillows featured here are made with a tapestry inset and a coordinating border fabric. Decorative gimp trims the border, and twisted cording, knotted at the corners, trims the outer edge.

Although the tapestry pillows have an opulent look, they are basically sewn like the feed-bag pillows on page 51, with the tapestry insets measuring about two-thirds the size of the pillow form. To feature a pictorial scene in the tapestry, large pillow forms, 22" to 28" (56 to 71 cm) square, work best. In keeping with the luxurious quality of the fabrics, down pillow forms are recommended.

LIST of MATERIALS

- ▶ Tapestry, for the pillow inset.
- ▶ Coordinating fabric, for the border and pillow back, yardage varying with pillow size and fabric width; l yd. (0.95 m) is usually sufficient.
- ▶ Gimp trim; yardage is equal to twice the size of pillow form plus twice the size of inset plus 5" (12.5 cm).
- ▶ Decorative twisted cording, ½" (1.3 cm) in diameter, in cotton or rayon; yardage is equal to four times the size of pillow form plus 65" (165.5 cm) for the knotted corners.
- ▶ Down pillow form.
- ▶ Sewing machine needle in size 16/100.

CUTTING DIRECTIONS

For the tapestry inset, cut a square of fabric, 1" (2.5 cm) larger than the desired finished size of the inset; center the desired tapestry design from side to side and from top to bottom. To help visualize the look of the inset before cutting, place strips of paper around the design as shown below. The border strips and pillow back are cut during the construction process.

Decide where to cut the inset from the tapestry fabric, using strips of paper to frame out the desired design area. Place the paper strips at right angles to each other, taping them together to leave a square opening of the desired finished size for the inset. Add ½" (1.3 cm) seam allowance on each side; cut fabric square.

1 ...... Determine the cut width of the border strips as on page 52, step 1. Cut two strips from the border fabric and stitch them to upper and lower edges of the inset as on pages 52 and 53, steps 2 and 3; press the seams open.

2...... Place gimp trim on pillow front, with gimp centered over seam at upper border; using size 16/100 needle, stitch in place along both edges of gimp. Repeat at lower border.

3...... Cut remaining strips from border fabric and apply them as on pages 53 and 54, steps 4 and 5; press seams open. Stitch gimp trim over seams.

4...... Pin pillow front to fabric for pillow back, right sides together. Using pillow front as a pattern, cut pillow back. Stitch and turn pillow cover as on page 54, steps 7 and 8.

5...... Insert pillow form, pushing corners of pillow form into corners of pillow cover. Slipstitch opening closed.

continued

6...... Wrap and tie thread around the end of the cording, to prevent raveling. Hand-stitch the cording to one side of pillow cover, using running stitches; start with end of cording extended 1½" (3.8 cm) beyond the corner.

7...... Measure cording 16" (40.5 cm) beyond the next corner; pin-mark cording at this point.

8...... Continue stitching the cording around next side of pillow cover, starting at pin mark; leave loop of cording free at corner.

9...... Repeat steps 7 and 8 for the remaining corners and sides of the pillow cover. At final corner, cut the cording 15½" (39.3 cm) beyond corner; wrap and tie thread around the end of cording, to prevent raveling.

10.... Overlap ends of cording ½" (1.3 cm). Hand-stitch through both ends of cording, and wrap thread tightly around the ends.

11.... Knot cording at corners, close to the pillow. At final corner, conceal the overlapped ends of cording in the middle of the knot.

Needlepoint
PILLOWS WITH SHIRRING

An old piece of needlework, such as needlepoint, makes a decorative inset for a pillow. This round pillow has a shirred velvet border that complements the needlepoint and is trimmed with twisted welting.

If you select a twisted welting that twists in the opposite direction from the welting shown, interchange the use of the words "left" and "right" in steps 6 to 8.

The inset should measure about two-thirds the diameter of the pillow form. For example, for an 18" (46 cm) pillow form, the inset should be a 12" (30.5 cm) circle, and the finished shirred border should be about 3" (7.5 cm) wide.

LIST *of* MATERIALS

▸ Old needlework piece, such as needlepoint.

▸ Velvet or decorator fabric, for shirred border.

▸ Muslin.

▸ Decorative twisted weltings in ¼" (6 mm) and ½" or ⅝" (1.3 or 1.5 cm) diameters.

▸ Round pillow form.

CUTTING DIRECTIONS

Cut two circles from muslin, with the diameter of the circles ½" (1.3 cm) larger than the size of the pillow form; from the border fabric, cut the pillow back to this same size. Cut the needlework inset as in steps 1 and 2, below.

Cut the fabric strip for the shirred border, with the width 1½" (3.8 cm) larger than the desired finished width; this allows ½" (1.3 cm) ease for a softly shirred effect and two ½" (1.3 cm) seam allowances. The cut length of the border is equal to two times the circumference of the inset.

1...... Cut out a circle from paper equal to the desired finished size of inset; place over needlework project, so circle is centered on the design from side to side and from top to bottom. Pin paper in place. Stitch around paper circle.

2...... Stitch ½" (1.3 cm) outside stitched circle, using zigzag stitch, to prevent needlework from raveling. Cut inset just outside zigzag stitching, taking care not to cut stitches.

3...... Center the inset piece on the muslin circle; pin in place.

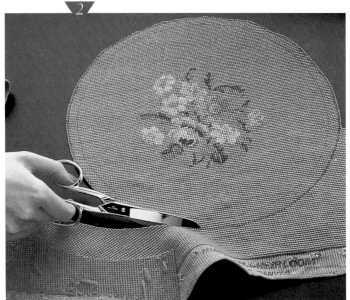

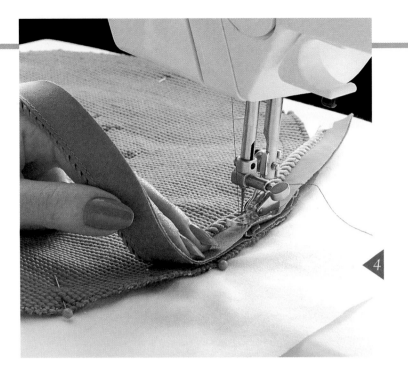

4...... Identify right side of the twisted
welting; from right side, inner
edge of tape is not visible. Baste
the twisted welting to inset, right
sides up, with cord along marked
seamline, using zipper foot; leave
3" (7.5 cm) tail at the beginning.
Wrap transparent tape around the
end of the tail to prevent raveling.

5...... Leave 1" (2.5 cm) unstitched
between ends. Cut the welting,
leaving 3" (7.5 cm) tail; wrap
end with tape.

6...... Remove the stitching from the
welting tape on tails. Trim the
welting tape to 1" (2.5 cm) from
the stitching; overlap ends, and
secure with tape. Arrange twisted
cording with the cording at right
turned up and the cording at left
turned down.

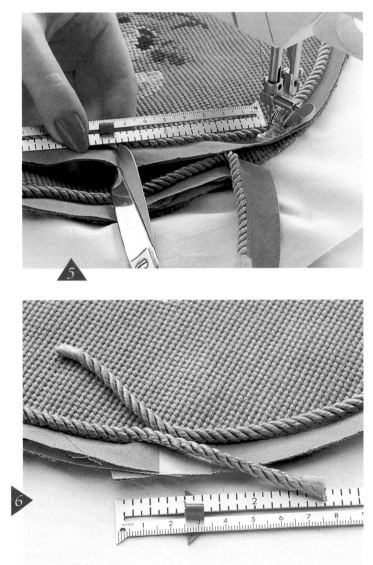

continued

7...... Insert cording at right end under the welting tape, untwisting and flattening it under the welting tape as shown. Secure in place, using tape.

8...... Place cording at left over cording at right until lapped area looks like continuous twisted welting; manipulate the cording as necessary, untwisting it partially to flatten it at seamline. Tape in place. Check the appearance on both sides of welting.

9...... Machine-baste through all layers to secure the welting at the seamline; use zipper foot, positioned so you can stitch in the direction of twists.

10.... Seam the border strips together to form a tube. Fold into fourths, right sides together; mark both of the raw edges at folds.

11.... Stitch gathering rows a scant 1/2" and 3/8" (1.3 and 1 cm) from each raw edge of border strip, using long stitch length.

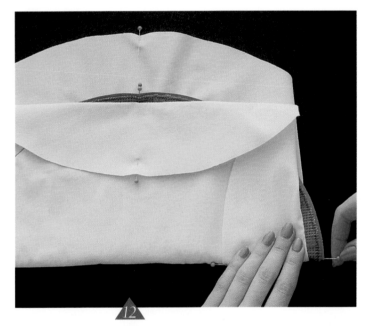

12.... Fold pillow top into fourths; mark folds at outer edge of pillow top and at welting.

13.... Pin border strip to pillow top, right sides together, with raw edge of border strip even with outer edge of needlepoint inset, matching markings.

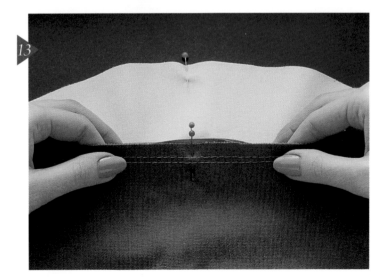

continued

14.... Pull gathering threads, and distribute the gathers evenly; pin in place. Stitch, using zipper foot.

15.... Pin outer edge of border to outer edge of muslin, right sides up, matching the markings. Pull gathering thread, distribute the gathers evenly, and pin. Machine-baste gathered border to muslin.

16.... Stitch twisted welting to outer edge as on pages 85 and 86, steps 4 to 9, with the right side of welting toward the right side of pillow top.

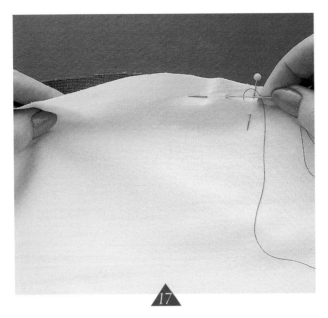

17

18

17.... Hand-baste the remaining muslin circle to the wrong side of the pillow back.

18.... Pin pillow back to pillow top, right sides together. Stitch ½" (1.3 cm) seam, leaving an opening for turning. Turn right side out.

19.... Insert pillow form. Fold under edge; pin and slipstitch the opening closed.

19

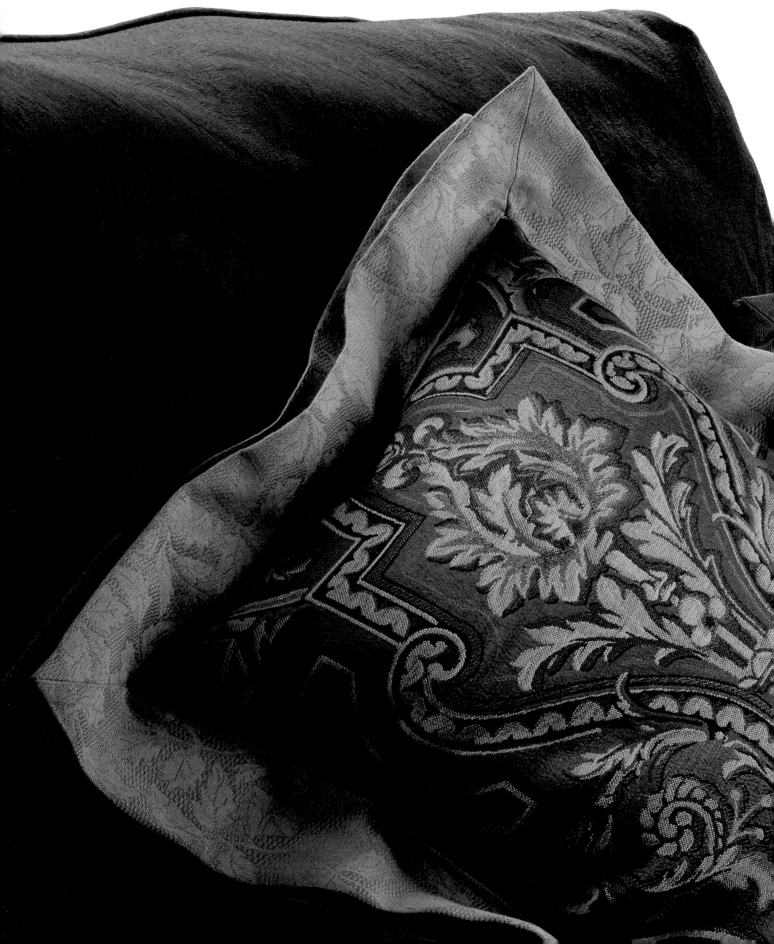

Double-flange PILLOWS

Double-flange pillows have an understated look and exceptional versatility. Made from brocades and tapestries, they are elegant in a traditional setting, yet their streamlined design makes them equally elegant in contemporary prints and solids. Select floral prints of polished cotton, and these pillows are right at home in a country room. For these pillows, two mitered panels are stitched together along the inner edge of the border, creating a double flange. At the center of the pillow, a matching or contrasting fabric is tucked under the flange before the pillow front and pillow back are joined.

LIST *of* MATERIALS

▶ Fabric for pillow front and pillow back, including flange, yardage depending on size of project; for 14" (35.5 cm) pillow form and 2½" (6.5 cm) flange, you will need ¾ yd. (0.7 m) of 54" (137 cm) fabric.

▶ Fabric for insert at center of pillow; yardage depending on size of project; for 14" (35.5 cm) pillow form, you will need ⅝ yd. (0.6 m).

▶ Pillow form in desired size.

▶ Polyester fiberfill, for filling out corners.

CUTTING DIRECTIONS

The size of the inner portion of the pillow is equal to the size of the pillow form. To this measurement, add four times the desired width of the flange plus ½" (1.3 cm) for turning under the raw edges; cut two pieces of fabric this size, for the pillow front and pillow back. For example, for a 14" (35.5 cm) square pillow with a 2½" (6.5 cm) flange, use a 14" (35.5 cm) pillow form, and cut two pieces, each 24½" (62.3 cm) square. For the center insert, add twice the desired depth of the flange to the size of the pillow form; cut one piece of insert fabric.

1...... Stitch scant ¼" (6 mm) from edges of the pillow front. Fold edges to the wrong side; press just beyond the stitching line. On each side, press under desired depth of flange.

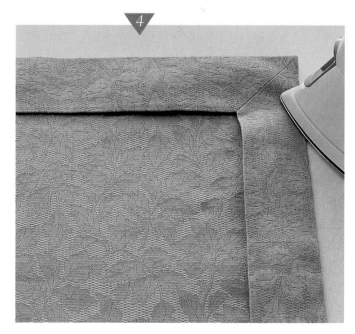

2...... Open out the corner; fold diagonally
so pressed folds match (arrows).
Press diagonal fold.

3...... Open out the corner. Fold through
center of corner, with right sides
together. Stitch on diagonal fold-
line from step 2. Trim the fabric at
corner ¼" (6 mm) from stitching.
Press seam open.

4...... Press the flange in place, turning
the corners right side out.

continued

5...... Place insert fabric on pillow front, tucking raw edges under flange; smooth, and pin in place.

6...... Press under sides of pillow back, an amount equal to the depth of flange plus 1/4" (6 mm), so fabric on folded flange is right side up. Miter corners as on page 93, steps 2 to 4.

7...... Place pillow front on pillow back, with mitered sides up, matching edges; pin.

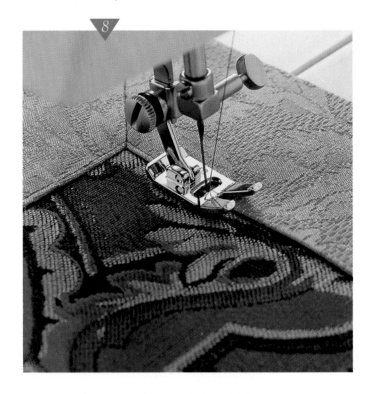

8...... Stitch around inner edge of flange, securing the insert; pivot at corners, and leave opening on one side for inserting pillow form.

9...... Insert the pillow form; push fiber-fill into the corners of the pillow as necessary to fill out pillow. Pin the opening closed; complete stitching on inner edge of flange.

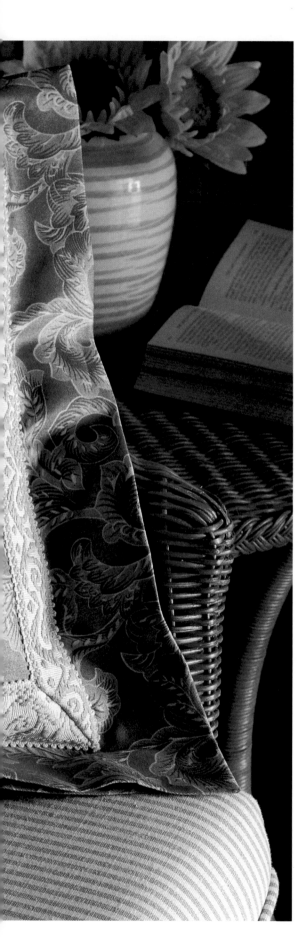

MORE IDEAS FOR
Double-flange
PILLOWS

The simple design of a double-flange pillow lends itself to a number of variations, as shown on the following pages. For additional impact, embellish the pillows with decorative trims. Weave ribbon trims together for an elegant checked effect, or apply them diagonally across the pillow front, creating a free-form pattern. For a different look, trim the inner edge of the flanges with a decorative braid trim.

The center portion of the pillow can have a pieced fabric insert for added interest. Select several coordinating fabrics, piecing them together in either a planned or random design.

DOUBLE-FLANGE PILLOWS WITH BRAID TRIM

LIST *of* MATERIALS

▶ Fabric for pillow front and pillow back, including flange, yardage depending on size of project; for 14" (35.5 cm) pillow form and 2½" (6.5 cm) flange, you will need ¾ yd. (0.7 m) of 54" (137 cm) fabric.

▶ Decorative trim, such as braid, for the inner edge of flange, length equal to perimeter of pillow form plus 2" (5 cm).

▶ Pillow form in desired size.

▶ Polyester fiberfill, for filling out corners.

CUTTING DIRECTIONS

Cut pillow front and pillow back as on page 92.

Braid trim, like the wide, elegant braid on this pillow, adds definition to the inner edge of the flange. The trim is mitered at the corners for a professional finish.

1...... Press flange and miter corners on both pillow front and pillow back as on page 94, step 6. Mark the finished width of flange on the unmitered side of pillow front, using chalk.

2...... Pin braid to pillow front, with outer edge of braid along marked lines; miter braid at corners by folding it at an angle. Fold end of braid diagonally at final corner; trim excess. Edgestitch along inner edge of braid.

3...... Pin pillow front and pillow back together with mitered sides facing. Edgestitch along the outer edge of braid, leaving an opening for inserting pillow form; hand-stitch mitered corners in place.

4...... Insert the pillow form; push fiber-fill into the corners of the pillow as necessary to fill out the pillow. Pin the opening closed; complete stitching on outer edge of braid.

DOUBLE-FLANGE PILLOWS
WITH DIAGONAL TRIM

LIST *of* MATERIALS

▶ Solid-color or reversible fabric for the pillow front and pillow back, including the flange, yardage depending on size of project; for 14" (35.5 cm) pillow form and 2½" (6.5 cm) flange, you will need ¾ yd. (0.7 m) of 54" (137 cm) fabric.

▶ Trims, such as ribbons.

▶ Pillow form in desired size.

▶ Polyester fiberfill, for filling out corners.

CUTTING DIRECTIONS

Cut pillow front and pillow back as on page 92.

Diagonal trims are positioned randomly for a creative effect. The printed fabrics used for these pillows reverse to solid black on the wrong side, making the contrasting flanges.

HOW TO SEW A *DOUBLE-FLANGE PILLOW* WITH DIAGONAL TRIM

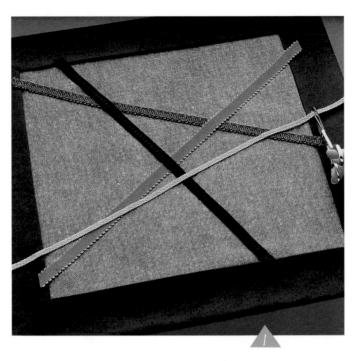

1...... Follow steps 1 to 4 on pages 92 and 93. Plan the placement of trims. Cut the trims to the lengths needed, allowing ¼" (6 mm) seam allowances.

2...... Secure trims to the pillow front with glue stick, tucking raw edges under flange. Stitch in place along edges of the trims. Complete the pillow as on pages 94 and 95, steps 6 to 9.

DOUBLE-FLANGE PILLOWS
WITH WOVEN INSERTS

LIST *of* MATERIALS

▶ Fabric for pillow front and pillow back, including flange, yardage depending on size of project; for 14" (35.5 cm) pillow form and 2½" (6.5 cm) flange, you will need ¾ yd. (0.7 m) of 54" (137 cm) fabric.

▶ Trims, such as ribbons or braids.

▶ Pillow form in desired size.

▶ Polyester fiberfill, for filling out corners.

CUTTING DIRECTIONS

Cut pillow front and pillow back as on page 92.

Cut trims 1" (2.5 cm) longer than measurement of pillow form; this allows sufficient length for ¼" (6 mm) seam allowances and for weaving the trims.

Woven insert made from iridescent ribbons adds impact to a double-flange pillow.

HOW TO SEW A *D*OUBLE-FLANGE PILLOW WITH A WOVEN INSERT

1...... Follow steps 1 to 4 on pages 92 and 93. Plan placement of trims. Apply glue stick to ¼" (6 mm) seam allowance at one end of each vertical trim; secure to pillow front, tucking seam allowance under flange. If necessary, trims may be spaced slightly apart.

2...... Secure horizontal trims to the pillow front as for vertical trims in step 1. Weave trims together; secure remaining ends of trims under flange, trimming any excess length to ¼" (6 mm) seam allowances. Complete pillow as on pages 94 and 95, steps 6 to 9.

DOUBLE-FLANGE PILLOWS
WITH PIECED INSERTS

LIST *of* MATERIALS

▶ Fabric for pillow front and pillow back, including flange, yardage depending on size of project; for 14" (35.5 cm) pillow form and 2½" (6.5 cm) flange, you will need ¾ yd. (0.7 m) of 54" (137 cm) fabric.

▶ Scraps of several fabrics, for pieced insert.

▶ Pillow form in desired size.

▶ Polyester fiberfill, for filling out corners.

CUTTING DIRECTIONS

Cut pillow front and pillow back as on page 92.

Pieced insert can be sewn in either a planned design or in a random, patchwork design.

HOW TO SEW A *D*OUBLE-FLANGE PILLOW WITH A PIECED INSERT

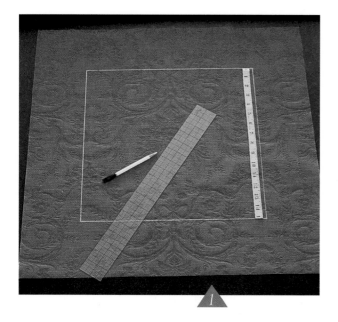

1 ...... Mark square or rectangle, 1"
(2.5 cm) larger than pillow form,
on wrong side of the pillow front,
centering it on the fabric.

2 ...... Cut a patch of fabric, and place
in center or corner of the marked
area; pin in place. Place a second
patch on the first patch, right
sides together, aligning one edge.
Stitch ¼" (6 mm) seam along
aligned edges.

3 ...... Flip the second patch right side
up; press. Pin in place. Continue
to attach patches until marked
area is covered.

4 ...... Sew pillow as on pages 92 to 95,
omitting step 5.

Ruffled

PILLOWS

Ruffled pillows are a perfect accent for a bedroom. Instructions are given for rectangular, square, or round pillows with either plain or stuffed ruffles. The rectangular and square pillow covers are made with a zipper closure so they can easily be used as pillow shams on bed pillows. Make smaller pillows as accents for bedrooms, sun rooms, or family rooms. If desired, a welting strip can also be inserted into the seam with the ruffle for additional interest. Make and apply the welting as on page 49, if desired.

Ruffled bed pillows (opposite) from back to front include pillow covers with self-fabric ruffles and contrasting welting, pillow covers with stuffed ruffles and welting trim, and a round accent pillow with a plain ruffled edge.

LIST *of* MATERIALS

▶ Decorator fabric.

▶ Zipper.

▶ Cord, such as pearl cotton, for gathering.

▶ Pillow form.

CUTTING DIRECTIONS

For a rectangular or square pillow cover, determine the finished size of the pillow cover by measuring around the pillow for length and width (above) and dividing each of these measurements by two. The cut length and cut width of the cover front is 1" (2.5 cm) wider and longer than the finished size. Cut the cover back the same width as the front, and 1½" (3.8 cm) shorter than the front. Cut a zipper strip 3½" (9 cm) wide and the same length as the cut width of the back.

For a round pillow, cut two circles from fabric, with the diameter of the circles equal to the diameter of the round pillow form plus 1" (2.5 cm) for seam allowances.

For the ruffle, cut fabric strips on the crosswise or lengthwise grain, with the combined length of the strips two or three times the distance to be ruffled, allowing for double or triple fullness. The width of the strips is two times the finished width of the ruffle plus 1" (2.5 cm) for seam allowances.

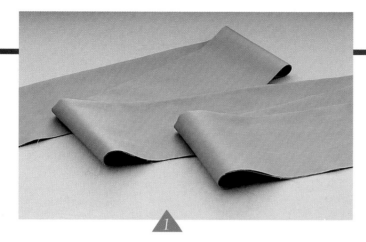

1...... Stitch fabric strips for the ruffle together in ¼" (6 mm) seams, right sides together. Stitch the ends of the ruffle strip together, forming a continuous strip. Fold the pieced strip in half lengthwise, wrong sides together; press.

2...... Zigzag over the cord a scant ½" (1.3 cm) from the raw edges. For more control when adjusting the gathers, zigzag over a second cord, within seam allowance, ¼" (6 mm) from first cord.

3...... Divide the ruffle strip and distance to be gathered on the pillow cover front into fourths; pin-mark. Place the ruffle strip on the pillow cover front, right sides together, matching the raw edges and pin marks; pull gathering cords to fit. Pin in place; stitch.

4...... Serge or zigzag along upper edge of zipper strip and lower edge of pillow cover back. Press finished edge of the zipper strip under ½" (1.3 cm), and finished edge of the back under 1" (2.5 cm).

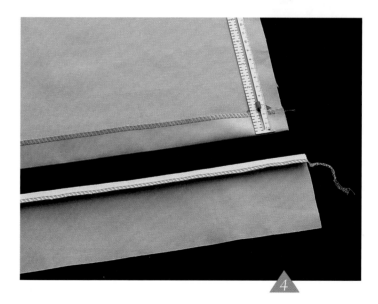

continued

5...... Place closed zipper facedown on seam allowance of the back, with edge of zipper tape on fold. Using zipper foot, stitch along one side of zipper.

6...... Turn right side up. Place pressed edge of zipper strip along edge of zipper teeth on other side of the zipper, and stitch close to edge. Backstitch at the end of zipper.

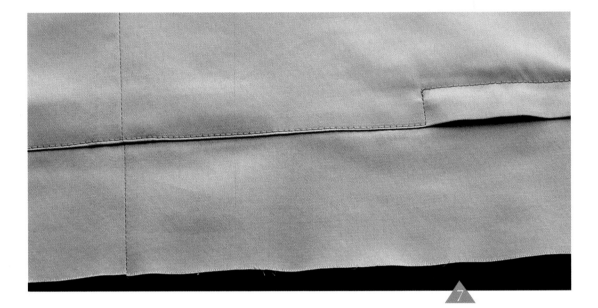

7...... Stitch across end of zipper; top-stitch through all layers to stitch seam from zipper to side of pillow cover. Repeat to stitch from other end of zipper to opposite side. Open zipper. Pin front to back, right sides together. Stitch inside previous stitches. Turn right side out. Insert pillow form.

Round pillow. Follow steps 1 to 3 on page 109. Pin front to back, right sides together. Stitch around the pillow cover inside previous stitches, leaving an opening for turning and inserting pillow form. Turn right side out. Insert pillow form. Slipstitch opening closed.

HOW TO MAKE A *P*ILLOW COVER WITH A STUFFED RUFFLE

LIST *of* MATERIALS

▶ Decorator fabric.

▶ Zipper.

▶ Upholstery batting.

▶ Cord, such as pearl cotton, for gathering

▶ Pillow form.

CUTTING DIRECTIONS

For a rectangular or square pillow cover, cut the front, back, and zipper strip as for pillow cover with ruffle (page 108). For a round pillow, cut the front and back pieces as on page 108. Cut fabric strips for the ruffle on the crosswise or lengthwise grain, with the combined length of the strips two times the distance to be ruffled, allowing for double fullness. The width of the strips is two times the finished width of the ruffle plus 2" (5 cm). Cut strips of upholstery batting, with combined length of strips equal to the finished length of the ruffle plus 3" (7.5 cm) for each corner. The width of the batting strips is 1½" (3.8 cm) less than the finished width of the ruffle.

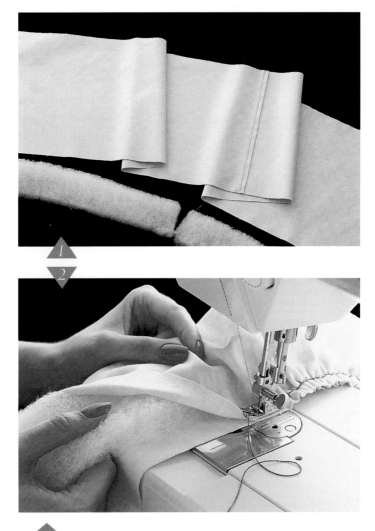

1 ...... Stitch fabric strips for the ruffle together in ¼" (6 mm) seams, right sides together. Whipstitch ends of batting together, forming continuous strips.

2 ...... Fold ruffle strip in half lengthwise, wrong sides together, encasing batting. Zigzag over cord a scant ½" (1.3 cm) from raw edges, encasing batting; do not catch batting in stitches. Stop at 10" (25.5 cm) intervals, leaving needle down; gently pull up on batting and cord, gathering fabric behind needle. Distribute gathers evenly.

3 ...... Apply the ruffle as on page 109, step 3. Complete the pillow cover as on pages 109 and 110, steps 4 to 7.

Round pillow (stuffed ruffle). Follow steps 1 and 2 above. Follow step 3 on page 109, leaving an opening in stitching. Insert pillow form; slip-stitch opening closed.

INDEX

CREATIVE PUBLISHING international

President/CEO: David D. Murphy
Vice President/Editorial:
 Patricia K. Jacobsen
Vice President/Retail Sales &
 Marketing: Richard M. Miller

Creative Textiles®
PILLOWS
Created by: The Editors of Creative
Publishing international, Inc.

Group Executive Editor:
Zoe A. Graul

Managing Editor:
Elaine Perry

Editors: Dawn Anderson,
Linda Neubauer

Associate Creative Director:
Lisa Rosenthal

Art Directors: Mark Jacobson,
Stephanie Michaud

Copy Editor: Janice Cauley

Desktop Publishing Specialist:
Laurie Kristensen

Studio Services Manager:
Marcia Chambers

Publishing Production Manager:
Kim Gerber

Printed on American paper by:
 World Color
1 0 9 8 7 6 5 4 3 2

Creative Publishing international, Inc.
offers a variety of how-to books. For
information write:
 Creative Publishing international, Inc.
 Subscriber Books
 5900 Green Oak Drive
 Minnetonka, MN 55343